The
COMPLETE
MAN

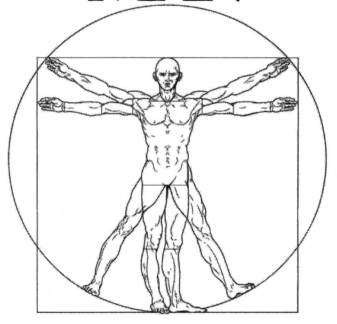

BY
GARY V CARTER

Published by: Kainos Enterprises
                  7777 Churchville Road
                  Brampton Ontario Canada L6Y 0H3
                  www.thecompleteman.today
ISBN-13: 978-1502800220

Contents

1. The Complete Man Is Not Yet Perfect

Nobody's perfect. I've got that point. Not you. And certainly not me. That is obvious so why would anyone use it as a justification for specific failures? Why would anyone settle for being less than they could become?

This book is for men. Men who know how imperfect they are and know that they are yet blind to many of their own imperfections. It is for men who are actually hiding some of their imperfection because they know something of the garbage in their souls.

Maybe you are stuck with the illusion that you can hide in the middle of the pack and be as good as the next guy. Shame! Who ever wants to march down Main Street chanting "We're Number 6!" with a crowd. At the beginning of the year does any team set their sights on being sixth in the B league? Ridiculous.

Men, we are wired to be the best we can be. Some of us may end up being bench warmers on the sixth team in the B league. But there is no shame in that if we strive to be all we can be.

Ladies, oh yes I know you are lurking in the background reading this book wondering if you should take the chance to read it to your men. In fact, sadly guys, more women will read this book than men. But I am going to pretend you aren't here ladies. Except permit me a few observations for women as we begin.

Ladies, you want the man in your life to be all he can be. Right? The very best thing you can do to move your man forward is to use fewer words and better behaviour. That is exactly what the Apostle Peter figured out. We know Peter was married because the Bible mentions his mother-in-law. But we don't know anything about his wife. I'm guessing that Peter got so much done in his life because of his wife. Realize Peter wasn't perfect. He had a habit of saying stupid stuff at the beginning. I'm just guessing. But I doubt that Peter's wife pointed that out to him every time he messed up. Why would I guess that? It is because toward the end of his life he gave some advice to women that has stood the test of time.

Here it is. *"Be good wives to your husbands, responsive to their needs. There are husbands who, indifferent as they are to any words about God, will be captivated by your life of holy beauty. What matters is not your outer appearance – the styling of your hair, the jewelry you wear, the cut of your clothes – but your inner disposition.* (1 Peter 3:1-4 MSG)

Ladies, please continue to read. And I would be very happy if you pass the book along. But never forget you aren't perfect either!

Now, back to you men. That passage from Peter talked about beautiful women. Now we are going to move on to attractive men. There are a host of other things to say than what I have to say here. It was hard to leave some important things out. Each chapter stands on its own and there is no particular sequence. My objective is to get you on the road to becoming more complete. I want to get you on the road of striving for perfection. I want you to be all you can be. And so do you. Believe that you can be more complete.

It takes less than ten minutes to read a chapter. You can do that. Start taking about ten minutes a day for a month thinking about these things and you will be amazed at how much the women around you start to look at you with admiration!

2. The Complete Man Loves

The rock star screams "I love you!" in front of an arena full of delirious fans. There is a connection but it is hardly love. It is so easy to translate an emotional connection to the word "love."

Some guys wonder why the words don't land like they used to with the people and especially the woman in their life. Let's figure that out.

Love is something you do. Sometimes it is nice to back that up with words. Sometimes flowers are a good add on. But the key demonstration is something you do.

Love is the setting aside of other choices in favour of acting in a way the person loved appreciates. When you love someone you actually look out for their interests more than your own. Sometimes you will simply not have time for the things you wish you could do. And that's OK if you really want to show love. There will be time for yourself later.

Most of the rest of this book points to the kinds of action a loving man is known for. It is not possible to cover all the bases in one book or twenty for that matter. But this will give you a good start if you actually want to be a good lover.

For this chapter let's look at this connection between emotions and love. When the human brain releases certain chemicals it leads to the emotions of fondness, attraction, appreciation, sexual attraction and other sensations we connect with the word "love." All these emotions are good and feeling good is good! But love is more than "a second hand emotion" (apologies to Tina Turner). Love has everything to do with it!

The first thing a man has to do about love is live it. Feeling it comes later. Sometimes feeling it may not come at all. When the loving actions have an embedded hook to get something from someone people figure you out. In particular, when you want to impress that woman in your life be it your sister, your mother, your wife or your date, when she figures out that you are being nice because you want something her skeptic gene will kick in and she will be resistant to you. Then if you blow your cover by going on some rant about what you did that wasn't appreciated she will know for sure that you don't really love her.

Figure out what to do that needs to be done. That is love. Don't spend your psychic energy on figuring out what to do to manipulate to get the results you want. Just figure out what to do. In order to get that to happen you need to listen for the clues along the road of life. Listen for the wishes and hopes. Then at a different time deliver on them when you can before you are asked.

Make a concentrated effort to separate your feelings from the acts of love in terms of your decision making process. Then you might just be surprised at the results from the emotional side of your life. Quit screaming, "I love you!" from the stage and do the things that need to be done. This will make you a more complete man. Get started on changing the way your brain is wired now. It will be worth it more than you could ever know!

3. The Complete Man Communicates

Communication is a two way street. Good communication involves taking in information and sharing information with others.

Communication is a difficult two way street to navigate. On the one hand communication includes talking. On the other hand communication involves listening. But on both hands communication involves the unspoken ways in which you communicate with your manner, tone and body language. It also involves the communication that comes across through the things you do to demonstrate that you are the true communicator.

You don't become a good communicator overnight. It takes practice. It takes discipline. It takes observation. It takes change.

Perhaps the basic lesson about communication is to just do it. Complete explanations aren't necessarily the heart and soul of good communication. The number of communication touches achieves more than the content of the communication for a woman. Quick phone calls and text messages initiated by the man in a relationship become very meaningful to the females in his life.

My guess is that it was some woman who invented text messaging. Two word sentences keep the communication ball rolling. Personally, I don't do well with this. In fact, I can barely say hello in the 140 characters allowed by Twitter. I like longer conversations better. When not much is going on it doesn't seem valuable to me to make a phone call to my wife that lasts about three sentences to tell her that not much is going on. I have to slap myself on the side of the head to remember that Wendy likes to know about the little details as they are happening. Text messaging may have been invented by women but men would be well advised to use the tool. If I had my life to live over again with the tools of today and if I were a better man, I think I would be texting my wife and daughters a whole lot more.

Complete men share what is in their heart. The most important and frequent communication between men and women must be between a man and his wife. Every time a man wanders from home it starts with too much communication between him and some other woman. Every man should save the deeper thoughts of his life for his wife. Certainly a man should talk with the other women around him. And sometimes those conversations may become long and meaningful but they must never become more important than the conversations between a man and his wife. Usually the wife will figure out if her man is talking too much with another woman before the man realizes it. She will notice that he is talking with her less. She may also start to notice that he isn't reporting as much on the conversations he has with the other women at work, at church or at the club. If your wife starts to tell you she is becoming concerned you are getting too close to someone, listen to her and correct your behaviour before it's too late.

This is a book addressed to men. But for a moment let's digress again. Ladies, it takes some time for men to share what is in the depths of their heart. Sometimes a man needs time to figure things out. Sometimes he needs to dump. Don't be too sure that anything is a final conclusion until it is stated as such. Thinking out loud is a good way to sort things out. You don't need to correct your man every time he says something he is feeling that isn't true from any objective standard. For example, when he tells you he is feeling worthless it isn't time for you to remind him of the long list of accomplishments of his life. Save that list for one-at-a-time reminders later on.

The complete man works on his communication skills. You might not start off well but you have to be bad at something before you get good at it. Struggle forward and let the words in your heart flow out even when it is hard at first. You can do this. Just try!

4. The Complete Man Concentrates

Getting things done requires you to pay attention. Men are particularly inept at paying attention when they don't have the desire to do so. On the other hand they are very good at paying attention if they want to. So the question really is about the desires the man experiences – not so much of his ability to pay attention. He can if he wants to.

It has been proven in recent years that the concept of multitasking or doing two things at once is actually a myth. Attempting to do so leads to time loss as the brain tries to figure out what to pay attention to first. Our brains can't do two things at once and so they attempt to schedule tasks one after the other. When we push hard to do many things at once the brain releases stress hormones which can cause long term health problems if not kept in check. Some people get very good at quickly changing their attention from one thing to the next to keep things in order. Some jobs require the person to do this many times in quick succession so that it appears they are doing two things at once but they aren't. They are actually causing wear on their system.

We get more done when we block out time to concentrate on one thing at a time. We might feel more engaged and productive living life based on inter-ruptions but it actually slows us down. When you are in a place where you have to pay attention to a lot of people in sequence things get hectic.

In a work place the phone might be ringing off the hook. You might be expected to respond to hundreds of emails and text messages in a given day. But you must remember to concentrate appropriately on each one that needs your attention. If you are too busy you have to find a way to communicate with others so they will know what level of responsiveness to expect from you. Ignoring people won't work well. If you need to ignore a question or conversation for a time you need to quickly say so to the other person. They will then know you have their concern in mind.

This need to concentrate in sequence is tough for a father in a home with several children. There are times when all the children want their father's attention all at once. They don't like to take turns telling their stories and asking their questions. But they can be taught to do so. The loudest voice must not dominate the time. You have to concentrate in fair balance with all the voices.

Some of the most blessed times in a man's life will come to him if he gets this right. He will have meaningful contact with many people outside the home and satisfying interactions at home. When the people in a man's life know they will get their turn and their fair share of time they are satisfied to wait for their time.

Everything will work out best if the man pays the attention he should to his wife. If she is constantly interrupting when his time is supposed to be allocated to other people there is something wrong. He can't simply drop his responsibilities every time his wife randomly comes up with something to ask or communicate. She will be more relaxed if she knows you concentrate on her when the time is right.

The habit of chasing mental distractions is a tough one to control. After all, so your wandering mind tells you, there might be something better than what you are supposed to be paying attention to. As with everything you need to change, start. The more you concentrate the better you will get at shutting out distractions. Over time you will become a champ if you try!

5. The Complete Man Is Balanced

The average guy is not a time waster in his own mind at least. He thinks all the stuff he does is important. An extra two hours on the Internet is reasonable in his mind. Buying the extra channels so he can see all the games is something he thinks he deserves. He is passionate about his toys, so he thinks, because the stresses of his job get him down. He thinks he will be cheated if he doesn't have some diversions. But you don't need to stay average.

It is true that the complete man is busy. And he manages that busyness to keep all aspects of his life in proper balance.

He doesn't give too much to his need to make a living. It is good that he cares about his job but with many jobs the work will never be done so there comes a time to walk away. Never walk away in the middle of a crisis or looming deadline. But get your headlights looking down the road far enough so you aren't slamming into more crises and deadlines. Learn to set realistic expectations for what you can handle.

As a general rule, estimate how much time something is going to take and then schedule double that time for the work. You may get it done in one and a half times the time you originally estimated but you are unlikely to meet your own expectations. Expect things to take longer than they should. Do high quality work consistently and meet the deadlines you set for yourself. Cooperate with others but be frank about what you can and cannot achieve. If you are the one who delivers the needed quality, others will have to wait for your timing. Three factors go together in the workplace. Everyone wants it with a low price, a high quality and in less time. It is hard to deliver on all three. Usually you get to pick one or two but not three elements. Remind your boss or your customers of that fact.

The complete man doesn't get lost in recreation. Relationships are destroyed when the man consumes too much time on anything that doesn't deserve the attention it is getting. It is way too easy to avoid what you should be doing in favour of an activity that gives you feelings of well-being, happiness or even euphoria. You will be able to find many accomplices if you want to run into a fantasy world of one kind or another. They are everywhere. You will find them in your current network of acquaintances or worse on the Internet.

The complete man doesn't neglect his family. And that includes his extended family – not just those in his home. When a man is married his first relationship is with his wife. The children must come after that. The same is true with grandparents. The grandchildren must not come first. When the relationships in the family get bumpy the complete man doesn't leave the solution development up to the woman. He participates in finding a unified and supportive approach. It isn't leadership when the man walks in and declares that since he is the head of the house he is determining the solution and declaring his right to impose it. He needs to take some leadership and be sure that solutions and even compromises when necessary are found. He can only do that by patiently listening to all perspectives while he does his thinking.

You don't achieve balance in fits and starts. When you get off course and over committed in some area you don't create balance by creating a pendulum swing to another extreme. It seems to me that often when a man gets out of balance by over committing in one area of life he backs off completely and creates an imbalance in another direction. You don't create balance by swinging the pendulum from one side to the other. You create balance by moving to the centre over time. Your credibility suffers dramatically if you do otherwise.

There will be times you need to say, "No" to others. But more often than not you need to say "No" to your own discretionary use of time. Balance is something you must work at every day. Don't wait. Move toward balance starting today.

6. The Complete Man Avoids A Lot

People are curious learners. We can't change that but we can control it. Indeed we must control what we learn. Mark Twain said, "A man who carries a cat by the tail learns something he can learn in no other way." In case you don't get it, carrying a cat by the tail is not smart unless you want to get bitten, scratched and clawed raw. The cat's tail may look like a convenient handle until you try it out.

Every day men grab some cat by the tail thinking it looks like a good idea. Some get killed by trying the convenient handles. Safety gear is a nuisance for real men you know. That is, until you learn the hard way why someone invented it. The same sense of invulnerability bleeds over into dabbling with attractive immoral choices. The cat tail is so easy to grab. A quick flirt or glance might be the cat's tail. Pictures of shiny objects the happy rich people have in the beer commercials might be the cat's tail. The lure of more money might wag in your face waiting for a quick grab.

There are three big cat tails you can learn about the hard way. Or you can take it from those who have gone before and figured out that they should be avoided. Remember these three Ss. One of them is going to get you if you are not careful. Sex. Sloth. Silver. You probably can figure out the details on your own. If it looks illicit it is. If it looks like the easy road it probably isn't. If it looks like a shortcut to riches take a hard second look.

The complete man exhibits self-control. He controls his mind, his mouth, his hands and his feet. By our fallen nature all these want to go in the wrong direction. When was the last time your child asked, "Can I clean my room now? Please!" Or when was the last time your teenage boy asked if he could come to the grocery store with you to help push the cart and get the groceries into the car for you? But that child's father if he is a complete man offers help like that. And his sons will have an example to follow.

We all want other people to control their thinking, their mouths, their hands and their feet. One of the things that goes wrong in people's lives, male and female alike, is that any sin starts in their mind. You think it before you live it. Stop it. The Apostle Paul said, *"We take captive every thought to make it obedient to Christ."* (2 Corinthians 10:5) Your mind will wander. There will be sinful options that will present themselves to you – ideas that stir up from within you.

Do you think there is any drug addict father in town who wants his little boy to grow up to be an addict? Do you think there is any mother who is a chain smoker who wants her little girl to grow up to be a chain smoker? They are going to copy you whether you like it or not. They won't do what you say; they will do what you do.

The only control you have jurisdiction over is self-control. So if you are feeling powerless realize you are not. You have work to do, as do we all. There are things to avoid no matter how attractive they may seem. Over time you will get better and better at it if you do your homework!

7. The Complete Man Faces A Lot

Life is hard and then you die. You've probably heard that before. It's more true than funny. When you look at others it may seem that their lives are exceptional and you are the only one who struggles. Or at least you might be trapped into believing that your struggle is more than the normal person's. Your struggles are different but probably not harder than the next guy's.

You find your relationships to be a struggle. Living with a wife isn't as easy as the engagement photo portrays. Don't let this shock you but living with you isn't so easy either. You just don't know what a jerk you can be. You aren't the exception; we all can be jerks at times. She is learning about that every day and if the damage hasn't cut too deeply she can teach you about it if you let her.

You find the people you work with to be somewhat troublesome. You see how they don't do what they should do. You get frustrated that they are so self-centred and oblivious to what is going on. Chances are really good that they think you are the one with the problem. How do you know they are not more right than you are? Insert some humility into your thought process.

You think you are a hero by dragging yourself out of bed on Sunday and shuffling out to the car to get to church. You might even warm the car up and sit there impatiently while she dresses the kids and gets her church face on. After all you are the king of the castle and the other dirty rascals should be grateful you quietly submit and go along. Are you under the illusion that the complete man behaves that way? Get a mentor and ask for a second opinion.

But the truly hard things are the ones that reside between the outer edges of your two ears. You face mood problems. You get discouraged. You get fearful. You get challenged. You get knots in your gut. You don't want to face hard conversations. You find words sneaking out from between your teeth that shouldn't be thought let alone spoken. In your mind at least you have a hard time keeping your zipper up. You explain away your own failure by pretending it was someone else who dropped the ball. And the worst thing is you keep bobbing and weaving, slipping and sliding so you won't get caught. Avoiding responsibility might just be the most wearisome thing you do. And you might not even realize it.

You would rather retreat to a fantasy world. You would rather take on an artificial challenge. You might shoot up the enemy on the screen and call that a stress buster. Really? Is that a true victory? So you got to a certain level in the game. Where in this world does that even matter?

So if any of the foregoing hard hitting questions or concepts cause you to realize there is a nasty truth in there somewhere what will you do about it? The complete man takes a look in the mirror, sees who he is and then puts a plan in place to change. This isn't a book with a focus on change. If you want to change get a good coach or mentor who will work with you and help you work on you. Nobody can change you; you have to change yourself.

The most beautiful thing is that Jesus and his people can support you in that change. Take full advantage. Compete against who you are, to become who you need to be.

8. The Complete Man
Shows Appreciation

Robert Louis Stevenson said, "The man who forgets to be thankful has fallen asleep in life." That seems like a simple concept. But so many simply run the red lights and don't even see them as opportunities to stop and show appreciation. The complete man finds different ways to show appreciation. He doesn't limit himself to "thankyouverymuch."

Appreciation can be demonstrated in many different ways. If you limit yourself to words and use them alone you are way above the average but you are still missing out. However, lets start with the words.

Words of appreciation can be used in the moment. Somebody does something good and you say thank you with a few sentences. Good start. Don't just think it; open your mouth. Remember to thank the important people in your life. It is possible to say thank you too often but very few people make that mistake. You are probably not one of those.

Try shaking your words up a bit. Actually, plan what you are going to say to communicate your appreciation. One great way to enhance your expression is to add the word "because" followed by a meaningful statement. That can show that your appreciation is more than just superficial words. Using "because" shows you have thought about it more deeply. Imagine for a moment that when the clerk says, "Thank you for shopping at _____ " and then adds "because ..." That would be a surprise wouldn't it? And if you are the clerk imagine finding another unique "because" for each client. "Thank you for shopping at _____ because it gives me the personal opportunity to help people and that makes me enjoy my work." Shocker huh? Then again what if on the other side of the counter you are the client and you say, "Thanks for bagging that up for me because it shows me you take your job seriously and I like to see people who enjoy their work." How often do you suppose that happens in a day? You can be the exception. That will give you good practice for when you get home and notice something a family member did that needs to be appreciated.

When you say thanks for something that others never notice it makes a positive difference. When you say thanks a day, a week or two weeks after the event that makes a very positive impression. Try separating the time you say thank you from when others are doing so. The week after a great meal is a time to say thank you for the memory created by the work to prepare the meal.

You can show your appreciation with cards, gifts, flowers or food. They are great ways to show you care. The thought counts much more than the actual tangible evidence. The more you match the tangible to the likes, wants and preferences of the recipient, the more it shows you really do appreciate the person. The greater the effort it takes for you to show the appreciation the more the demonstration will itself be appreciated.

When you start every day expressing your appreciation to the Lord for all he has done and continues to do, the stronger your ability to thank others. Life is a great gift in itself. Remembering to appreciate it demonstrates that you haven't fallen asleep.

9. The Complete Man Thinks

The human brain is made to think. In fact, you are thinking all the time – but you might not know it. Even when you are asleep your brain is still thinking. We know that because everyone dreams. You could be one of those who say they don't dream. Actually you do dream but you may not remember it when you awake.

When I was a boy I was scolded for daydreaming in school. I was taught that daydreaming was a bad idea. All I was doing was thinking about something else other than what the teacher thought I should be thinking about. It wasn't a problem to be sorting things out in my mind. It was a problem that I wasn't sorting out the correct things. I didn't want to solve the problems of boring schoolwork. I wanted to get on with building forts and hitting home runs. I hit many home runs in my head but not so many on the ball field. In fact, I don't recall ever hitting a home run in real life.

I have noticed that men who have a hard time hitting home runs in real life spend more time hitting them in video games. Winning a game isn't winning in life.

Complete men think a lot about winning in real life. They put their minds to solving problems at home, at church and at work but only a little on the sports field. Unfortunately, the challenges they think about are often not the ones that are most important. You have to ask yourself what you are thinking about or else you might be thinking about the wrong things.

If you are thinking too much about where to catch the big fish without remembering to buy the fish for dinner you are in trouble. Get your head into the correct space.

If you are spending too much time thinking about how to fix other people you may not be spending enough time thinking about how to fix yourself. You can't fix anybody but yourself. And besides, why would you want to fix anyone else anyway? Is it because you just want your own life to run with less stress and more ease?

If you are spending time thinking about how to get your own way, you are way off course. God didn't give you your mind so you could strategize how to manipulate the world to do things your way. He gave you your mind so you can figure out how to make the world a better place. Forget about the world. Think about how you can make your home a better place. And that could be as simple as cutting the grass before you are nagged to do so.

If you are thinking about completing your household chores or working on a hobby while you should be thinking about what your job requires of you, you are thinking about good things but at the wrong time. Sometimes life requires you to do repetitive work that doesn't require much thinking. That is a great time to get two things done at once.

It is commonly known that men think a lot about how they can get more sex. Even if you have a very active sex life it is only about 1% of your time. Why on earth would you waste the other 99% daydreaming about the 1%? Take control of your mind. Apply your mind to pleasing your spouse in sex when the appropriate time comes – not on how to get your spouse to please you. Women get exasperated when they realize their man is really only trying to get them in bed for their own pleasure. Women get really discouraged with a man who has that one track mind.

However, sometimes the problem is simply that you don't want to be forced to think. And in particular you might find it irritating to read something that forces you to think differently. But if you want to be a more complete man it will start with the way you think. And if you simply repeat the same thoughts over and over again you will not change; you will only dig a deeper rut.

If you don't want to grow and become a more complete man then nobody can help you. But if you do want to change you can find the help you need. You can change your patterns. Start now and stay with it.

10. The Complete Man Thinks Ahead

There are only a few important questions to think about when it comes right down to it.

The first question is the one most people get hung up on. It is, "Now what?" It is a very important question because the next step for your life will, as often as not, require some decision you didn't expect to face. It could be as simple as road construction blocking your path when you are already late. Now what? Your mind will buzz through the alternatives. Should I just get there when I get there and blame it on the unexpected construction? Should I call ahead and explain? Should I find another route?

How you answer, "Now what?" depends on how you have answered the other more important question. If you get the other main question sorted out in your mind based on what is valuable to you it limits the range of possible answers in the "now what" phase. That more important question is, "Then what?" For example, if you make a commitment to the standards we are discussing throughout this book it will simplify your options and lower your stress. When you make a commitment to yourself to tell the truth in all circumstances you won't just blame the road; you will accept responsibility for not taking reasonable precautions about the travel time and conditions. And you will usually do your best to minimize the stress of the people on the other end. That probably means you will pull off the road and give them a phone call. Simple.

However, life is more complicated than that. If you take every "now what" decision and track it out by answering "then what" first you will be far better off. Ask yourself where you want to be in the future – be that in 24 hours or 24 years and then make decisions for today based on the likely future consequences. You can guess where you will be in 24 hours, days or years and you may be right. Or you may be wrong. You can never know for sure but you can live in such a way that the consequences you face are much more predictable than not. For example, why does it take a heart attack to get the attention of some guys that their lifestyle and eating habits need to change? Nobody gets fat on one milkshake. But a super-sized burger, poutine, a milkshake and an ice cream dessert for lunch every day has consequences. Is there anybody who believes otherwise?

There is a third question you are always facing and we won't have the space to completely discuss it here but it is very important that you learn the skills to answer it properly. The question is, "What next?" This is the question you live with moment by moment and day by day. Once you finish the current action what will be the next thing? When you learn to anticipate the next task and manage it with your commitments and values you are well on your way to being a much more complete man.

It is a clear sign of immaturity for a man to be always planning the next goof off time and seek to order his life to get to the games and relaxation. Guys often do a half-hearted job at something just so they can get on to concentrating their attention of finding pleasure. What an immature waste to consume your planning on finding escape in pleasure. This shouldn't come as a shock to you but you don't deserve it. You don't work that hard and you know it.

It could be that your mate stuck this book in front of your face and told you to read it. Quite frankly, you might have been smart enough to know that it would not be in the best interest of your well-being in the household if you didn't at least read a little bit.

You must come to the process of reading with an open heart ready to learn how to change. Get on the road to completeness!

11. The Complete Man Thinks of Others

Be honest with yourself and answer the following question. "How much time do I spend thinking about how to please others?" Seriously. Think about the day so far. Did you give a rip about someone else and what they need? If you haven't done so, why not? Strong men think about how to build up the people around them. *"We who are strong ought to bear with the failings of the weak and not to please ourselves. Each of us should please our neighbors for their good, to build them up. For even Christ did not please himself."* (Romans 15:1-3)

Complete men don't consume their time complaining about the boss or the co-worker. When was the last time you did something nice and unexpected for your boss? For that matter, when was the last time you even said thank you to your boss? I expect you have thought about the fact that the boss seldom says thank you to you. But have you ever thought about saying thank you to your boss? The world doesn't owe you a living you know. Besides the people who get promoted are not those who complain about others in the workplace around them. The people who are promoted are the ones who think positively about contributing to the profitability and success of their business.

Furthermore, complete men don't come home after work and dump garbage all over their wives every day. Men, your wives have quite enough garbage to deal with on their own. That is not to suggest that you don't share your burdens with your wife. Your marriage will profit if you seek to discuss your work difficulties with each other with a mind to finding solutions and a better course. You need to communicate. You don't need to recycle garbage.

Thinking is not an automatic process. Most people consume their lives without ever considering what they are thinking about. They believe they have no control over what goes through their mind. But when you think about it, you realize that you choose the subject matter you let through the gate of your consciousness. You actually do decide the approach to the subject matter that is flowing through your brain. There are over two billion hits if you Google the phrase "how to think." Clearly, somebody out there is thinking about how to think and has written those words down to be published on the Internet.

If you want to impress the women in your life become a thinker. You will impress your daughters when you help them solve perplexing problems because you know how to think yourself and are willing to engage them in conversation. The respect you gain from your wife will rise if you come to her with possible solutions for something that is concerning her because you have thought them up in your own little head. And even your mother might be proud of you when she sees that you quit daydreaming and started to do something real and useful with the brain power God gave you.

Maybe you need to set an alarm on your phone for once an hour to notify you of the commitment you make. Just set the reminder with a question like this, "Is there someone I should be thinking of right now?" Develop a new set of habits and you will become like a new man.

12. The Complete Man Cares

When things get emotionally difficult or painful many men simply shut down and refuse to deal with the situation. Withdrawal usually isn't an attractive approach. Withdrawal creates uncertainty in the mind of the other person. In particular, when a man simply walks away from the situation it really makes the woman in his life feel insecure and undervalued. Rather than just running away a man who is feeling a lot of negative emotions rise can simply say, "I am really having a hard time keeping myself from saying things I will regret and that I don't really mean. I hope it will be OK with you if I just take some time to sort things out. But I promise I won't let this go; we'll pick up the conversation later. Will that be OK?"

The complete man has many family members to relate to. There are rare exceptions to that. Sadly, some men will suggest they have nobody in their family but neglect to explain they have burned all the bridges with the result that people don't want to relate to them anymore. Often this is a result of one or more explosive conversations where they have lost their temper and they are too proud to ask for forgiveness. When they are honest with themselves they can identify the defining moment when things broke down. Even if it was 25 years ago they can remember the event as if it was yesterday. Caring enough to restart the conversation will be very difficult. If you find yourself in that situation you need the help of wise counsellors who can help you sort out what to do, what to say and what not to say.

When a person has toxic relationships in their background it is very hard for them to get beyond those failures and relate properly to people in the present. It isn't always possible to restore broken relationships from the past but it is always possible to seek to understand those relationships and how history impacts the present.

This is a difficult part of life to manage on your own. It is particularly difficult for men who had a bad relationship with their fathers to develop solid relationships with other people in the present. In particular, they will often have a problem relating to the people who have authority over them. When the trust between a father and a son is broken it is far too common for the son to make a direct choice to never extend trust to another man. When you don't trust somebody you always are in danger of misinterpreting their motivations.

When a man really cares to have the kind of solid relationship with a life partner, a family member, a friend or a work mate he must invest a lot of energy in figuring out how to rebuild the way he thinks so that he can develop and maintain a wholesome rapport. The man who cares doesn't avoid the problem; he takes it head on. He gets help from a trusted mentor or coach and surrounds himself with emotionally healthy people who won't let him get away with his rationalizations crafted to deflect blame to others.

Show people how much you care by remembering their concerns and inquiring about their well being. Match your inquiry with some tangible action to help and your caring will rise off the charts.

13. The Complete Man Manages Inhibitions

An inhibition is an internal mechanism – some say feeling – that restrains a person from taking a particular action. Inhibitions are both good and bad. Without inhibitions we would all end up in train wrecks of one sort or another. Say the wrong thing and you can blow up a relationship or lose a job. Do the wrong thing and you can create a world of hurt. Most men can recall times in their youth where they did or said something really stupid. With proper inhibitions in place that stupid thing could have been eliminated. The sad part is that some men never grow up enough to put the right inhibitions or boundaries in place. You don't want to be one of those guys!

This is all about pre-thinking the fences, lines and boundaries you have in place. It is wise to build your schema of inhibitions based on thinking things through and not just adopting an inhibition based on prior experience.

For example, perhaps when you were a child you developed distaste for vegetables. Perhaps you were forced to eat things you simply didn't like and still carry uneasy feelings related to eating vegetables. So you still say, "No! I don't like that!" It is pretty certain, that inhibition is going to catch up with you and shorten your lifespan if you don't find a way to change your habits. You can learn to eat vegetables, you know. And your mother was correct; they are good for you. Think that through. Do you want to be healthy or would you rather not?

Men often find it difficult to express their thoughts for fear of getting emotional. Get in touch with your emotions and learn to express your thoughts to the right people at the right time and in the right way. The issue is not your thoughts and emotions but the inhibiting boundaries you have built that perhaps need to be rethought. Women love to know what men are thinking and feeling as long as the negative side doesn't explode into hurtful words and actions. When someone loses their temper it is because the inhibitions are not well managed. Words blurt past the filters and can never be taken back once said. When things bottle up inside the cork could burst at the wrong time in the wrong place with the wrong person.

Strong men are spiritual men who are willing and ready to explore what is going on inside of them with a level of personal vulnerability. This may not come naturally at first but it is a tremendously freeing experience for a man to talk about the truth inside with someone who cares and can provide perspective. If you are married this is conversation material between you and your spouse. Since you have a coach or mentor you have at least one man you can trust and explore your inner being with. Don't let fearful, inappropriate inhibitions hold you down because of some failed attempts at self-disclosure in the past.

I believe the wise man never opens the doors of his life to pathways that could lead to disaster. Marriages break up because one partner starts developing intimate conversations with someone other than their spouse. Just don't go there. Be inhibited. Lives are ruined because of the abuse of substances that alter the thinking processes. According to *Drug Harms in the UK* by David Nutt et al, published in *The Lancet*, "Overall, alcohol was the most harmful drug (overall harm score 72) heroin (55) and crack cocaine (54) in second and third places." To me it is simple. Never take a first drink and you will never have an alcohol problem. Be inhibited. What is more, you will never face the problem of a teenager in your house saying, "You do it; so why can't I? I'm an adult now you know." Nothing can cloud the other appropriate inhibitions of your life like a few drinks. Choose to be inhibited because you want to avoid disaster.

Take some time to figure out which inhibitors need to be reinforced and which ones need to be eliminated. This is a management task that reaps huge dividends when you take it seriously.

14. The Complete Man Loves Fun

Fun is good. Laughter is good. Joy is good. Smiling is good. When you wake up in the morning do you moan, "Grrr. Don't talk to me. I haven't had my coffee yet." It is uncommon for men to realize that they actually can control their moods. When situations are difficult then mood control is even more challenging but it is still totally the responsibility of the individual. It may take a minute or two after you choose to change your mood for the emotions to catch up but catch up they will if you take control. It really isn't about coffee.

When you tell yourself you are having a good day it takes your brain away from all of the bad things and lets you see the good things. When you are worrying, you won't notice the sunshine. When you are afraid, you might not see the sparkle on the water. When you are discouraged, you won't smell the green grass in the summer or see the whiteness of the snow in winter.

The psalmist taught us two very good lessons in this regard. He said, *"Why, my soul, are you downcast? Why so disturbed within me?"* (Psalm 42:5) The first thing to do when your mood is demonstrating bad attitudes is to give yourself a good talking to. You have to ask yourself the tough questions. The concern you think is really bugging you may actually only be a symptom of something far deeper in your life. So you have to ask the right questions of your own soul. Secondly, in the same verse the psalmist said, *"Put your hope in God, for I will yet praise him, my Savior and my God."* Whatever the problem you are facing, once you have analyzed what's going on inside, you need to deliberately turn away from that and go back to the bedrock of life. You see, for example, if you lose your job that you trusted in for many years it will put you in a deep funk if you can't move on to step two. If you don't find hope in God it will be a very long time before you get your momentum back, if ever.

Make life a joyful experience. Sometimes you have to stir yourself from deep down inside. You might have to fake it a little until your brain chemistry catches up. But if you can't find joy then it is pretty clear you have lost sight of Jesus. No doubt there will be some who read that sentence who really don't get its impact. For them, perhaps they think Jesus is just a bolt-on accessory that they could take or leave. Jesus said, *"I have come that they may have life, and have it to the full."* (John 10:10) Do you think he was lying? If not, then you can find a full and happy life regardless of the circumstances.

It is all too easy for a man to come home from work as a grouch. Things go wrong in every work place. Co-workers often are a source of irritation. Don't take it out on the people in your house. Decide to change your mood and pretend to be nice and fun loving. You will be amazed at how pretending what you want to become moves you in the direction of the mood change you need.

Develop things to do that are fun for every other person you live with. Learn to like what they like. Repetition of something you don't particularly like over time will become familiar and you might get to like it in spite of yourself! Learn to play in the way the others want to play. And that goes for spouses as well. Make your life fun by having fun with others on their terms – not by trying to get them to like your kind of fun.

You have got to develop a sense of humour to experience it. You can learn to see the funnier side of life.

There are a huge number of lies the people around you believe about good times. Just look at the after burn and you will realize they really aren't too smart. We all can have the most fun being sober, upright and moral. Jesus said so. Believe it!

15. The Complete Man Reads

Many men will tell you they simply don't read. But what is worse, they have no intention of changing their lives so they do read. It is common for men to spend many hours taking in information off a screen. At home the screen will probably be one broadcasting video or social media. At work the screen could be showing data concerning instrument readings, words or numbers. Much information is placed in your hand with a mobile device of some sort. So when you broaden the definition of reading to take in all forms of information it is clear that men do read. Sometimes they like it; sometimes they don't.

In the workplace it may be that the material they must read is for the purpose of expanding their knowledge, understanding or skill related to their job. That is work. They have to do it or not come away with a pay cheque. Sadly, the worker may not find this sort of reading interesting, fulfilling or engaging.

At home their reading is often for the purpose of entertainment to distract them from their real world. Sometimes the reading is simply playing a video game. Violent video games really bother me because they seem to tap into a fantasy world built around aggressive behavior. Aggressive behavior is seldom seen as attractive by women. So what the women in your life really want seldom includes you watering the weeds of violence in the inner seedbed of your soul. On top of that, wasting time in a fantasy world leaving household chores or repairs undone is hardly a license to impress the women in your life. It has to be a form of insanity to believe that the male has the right to fritter time away while the female in the home has to take care of more detail to keep their refrigerator full of food and the drawers full of clean laundry. You don't have a moment to waste. There is time to rest but never time to waste. Instead of eating up those never to be returned minutes with distraction it makes much more sense to use those minutes to build your life habits with wholesome reading that is productive.

Grant Cardone, a prominent best selling author and speaker asserts that the average CEO is said to read over 60 books a year and makes 319 times the income of the average worker who reads one book a year but finds the time to watch 700 YouTube videos a year. I don't know where he got his numbers but it makes sense to me. My life experience tells me that the people I gravitate to are those who are further ahead than I am in their understanding of life. Invariably these people do a lot of reading.

Of course there's only one chief executive officer in every entity and it is foolish to assume that every reader could fulfill that role in their world. However the principle is that those who get to the top get there by reading a lot.

You don't need to compare yourself to anyone else. Just compare who you are today to the man you want to become tomorrow. Then start moving in the right direction. One step at a time is all it takes.

16. The Complete Man Is Interesting

When you can carry on intelligent conversations on many subjects you start to become an interesting person. You don't simply get interesting by only knowing the sports scores and watching the latest viral video. Few people will find you interesting if you just pay attention to the things that interest you. You have to learn to be curious about many things.

Let's go back to the beginning. It comes down to the desire that rests in all of us to learn more and more. We call it curiosity. The old saying suggests that curiosity killed the cat. Maybe. But lack of curiosity kills people. Curious people take in information by reading in the broad sense. If you are a man who doesn't like to read there have to be some underlying reasons. First of all we have to settle the fact that you actually can read; you just choose not to. So the question is why don't you read? Women have a tendency to read for relaxation and distraction. Sometimes men read for simple relaxation as well but that is not what I have in mind here.

The kind of reading I am talking about is the kind that will fill your mind with useful, positive thoughts and concepts that will make you a more complete man. Why wouldn't you want to read? It could be that you actually want to fill your mind with good stuff but that you find it difficult to take the words off the page and translate them into understanding in your heart and mind. It stands to reason that if you have not read in the past you will find it more difficult in the present to assimilate information off the printed page. You can get better at it by practicing. And in the interim you can get an app for your phone that will read things to you. So you are without excuse because you can listen instead of reading and get the same results.

You don't have to read a book all at once. If you set your mind on reading for ten minutes a day you can make a serious difference in your life. Within a few short weeks those around you will notice that you seem more intelligent, purposeful and peaceful if you will simply pick up something good to read almost every day. A one hour prime time television program has about 20 minutes of commercials. Many times the same commercial is repeated several times during that one hour. Don't just mindlessly sit there and watch it again. Turn down the volume and read for two or three minutes. At the end of an hour you should be able to fit in ten minutes of decent reading. Probably you will lose your place and have to go back a bit each time you start up again. So what? You will get your reading value in if you simply push yourself to do it. That shouldn't be the end of your reading experience but it could be a start.

You can watch informative television to "read." You can track with the world news as part of your reading. You can go to museums and lectures. It goes on and on. So when I use the word "read" it is much more than words on a page; it is using the magnificent capacities of language and observation to expand your mind.

When you expand your mind and choose wholesome experiences you become much more dynamic. You then develop ability to connect with other people at points of interest that they care about.

You will only become more interesting when you have something to say. When someone asks, "What's new?" they aren't impressed with "Not much." However, when you can tell them something they usually love it. You can become like the old town crier who always had some new information.

Learn something new every day that is useful in some way. Chances are it will be something you use within a day or two. Now that is interesting.

17. The Complete Man Befriends Others

Everyone knows we are supposed to be friendly. It sounds simple enough. At the same time it is commonly understood that men seldom have true friends. In fact, the subject is so important that a book *The Friendless American Male* by David W. Smith became a best seller a generation ago. And things are just as bad today or even worse.

Perhaps men are more conscious to pay attention to their wives and family than they used to and leave their workplace on time. I am not sure about that. But I am sure their friendships with men are often very superficial. They get together to watch the big game or go golfing or fishing together. But when the chips are down few friends are to be found.

Guys who are complete men are a help to their friends. They stand beside their friends when the going gets tough. There are many ways they prove their friendship.

You know you are a friend when you say "Yes!" to a request. You don't complain about how busy you are and make your friend shy away from ever asking again. When a friend calls for help you say "Yes" first and then figure out how to rearrange your schedule second. You only think you don't have the time. But when you become a true friend you find there is time for everything you need to do.

It goes further. When you are a true friend you see the need in another man's life and offer to put in the time to get him over a hump. He may not even see his own hump. For example, you might overhear his wife talk about the need to clean out the yard or the garage. You see, your friend will often delay because he doesn't know where to begin. That is when a true friend jumps in and asks, "What are you doing next Saturday morning starting at 7 a.m. because I will come and help. It will be a blast!"

Often what guys need is a listening ear. When you see the temperature rising in a friend's life you can position yourself so your friend can talk about it with you. Careful. If you go at it directly and ask, "Do you need to talk?" he might simply say, "No. I'm good." After all men are tough, right? Not so much. But if you just show up with an extra coffee in your hand on a Saturday morning maybe the conversation starts.

How will you fit in the extras here? That depends on your schedule. If you have commute time you can use it to talk hands free on your phone. You can even sneak in a quick call while shopping or watching a child's game. You can send a quick email first thing in the morning or a quick text message to someone who needs your touch.

Great friends do these sorts of things during the course of the regular affairs of living. The best way to have friends is to be a friend to others. Over time friendships can grow if you build the habit of making regular contact. You can be the friend someone desperately needs. And in befriending someone who needs a friend you gain one for yourself.

18. The Complete Man Puts Up With A Lot

Tolerance is a tricky subject. Everyone wants you to be tolerant of the issues they believe should be tolerated but willing to take a stand against practices they believe should be rejected. Of course, you don't see things exactly the way others see them. Therefore, you are going to disagree with everyone on something. The issue is how you disagree without being disagreeable.

There is a difference between giving someone authorization to live in a certain way and tolerating how they live even though, if asked, you would never give permission.

There are various levels of tolerance. You have no opportunity to control how any other person lives if they don't live under your roof. If you own the roof over someone's head you do get to set some house rules about what they do in your space but that of course is very limited as well. This means that you do have something to say about what is acceptable behavior with your family members. Even then, as your children grow and establish more and more independence they will choose their own set of standards for life. You can encourage them to live in a certain way but when they don't, you have to find a way to tolerate their differences.

It is important to establish the fact that while you might have firm convictions about some moral standards it isn't possible to control the society and how they live. You can establish your own self-control.

It is a good thing to play together and to play fair. I have noted that the people who have the hardest time getting along in the workplace and in the church are the people who had the hardest time getting along with their own siblings in the home. Perhaps they grew up at a distant age from other children, were alone in the family or were from a blended family that didn't mix well. They still believe as adults that everything should go their way.

Tolerance tends to grow over time for the wrong reasons. People tend to say, "Who am I to say? I have my own problems." That's not the reason for tolerance. Tolerance isn't a question of lowering the standard. It is a question of opening up your heart and your mind. Mothers always want their children to exhibit a degree of tolerance that matches their self-control. When did you ever, as a child, go to your mother and confess, "Mom, I'm so sorry. I got into a fight with my sister/brother and I started it." Who started the fight? You never started it, right? That can't be true, can it? But you claimed it as truth. It has never been easy to tolerate somebody occupying your space, borrowing your things and not returning them. Tolerating is not authorizing. You don't need to roll over and declare, "OK take all my stuff or invade my space." But you do need a tolerant attitude for others. Back in the day, parents used to kick the kids outside to go settle their own disputes. That's sort of a good strategy since you have to learn to get along with other people sooner or later.

The complete man has a high level of tolerance for irritants. He doesn't get angry over failed expectations. But he does show his disappointment at the right time because he wants to help others learn the art of tolerance.

If you find yourself becoming irritated just remember how much you dislike others being irritated with you. Cut people some slack. Treat others the way you yourself wish to be treated. Jesus said, *"Do to others as you would have them do to you."* (Luke 6:31) That is known as the Golden Rule. It only works when you accept the fact that you are it!

19. The Complete Man Is Consistent

One of the biggest complaints I have heard over the years is that a particular person is unpredictable and you can't count on them. It may be that they do what they are supposed to do four days out of five. In their own mind that might be a success. It won't be viewed as a success in the workplace and it shouldn't be seen as success in any other area of life.

You have to show up. You have to show up on time. You have to show up prepared. You have to show up without excuses. These responsibilities escape some men. They think that what they got away with in grade school should still be true today. It is true that some men who are exceptionally charming get away with more than they should. But do they really get away with it? When people start saying of you, "That's just the way he is" you are in trouble.

For some, sad to say, the only consistent characteristic about them is their inconsistency. But those who are consistently inconsistent explain themselves to themselves as free. They probably have been watching too much TV with some gun slinging hero from the old west as their idol. He could roam and untangle any mess he got into with bravado. That makes for colourful television but doesn't work in real life.

For others, equally sad to say, it is they are consistently rigid. Total predictability leads to absolute boredom. It could be that their adolescent insecurities solidified them on what they see as a safe path. With pride they hold to their compulsive tendencies as the high road others should walk. That kind of consistency is entirely unattractive. If that is you, there is a good chance the world is laughing at you behind your back.

So what is the consistency you want to develop? You want people to know you are the man who will set aside his personal desires to meet the needs of others. They want you to take the lead or take a stand when things go bad. People are confident in men who don't wimp out.

A consistent man shows up for the people in his life. If married his wife knows that he will be there for her when he is needed. His children know that he will drop virtually anything for them when he should be there for them. There will probably be times when he will have to take care of some other responsibility because the circumstances demand it. But those he loves know that while they might be set aside for a moment they can count on their man to be back to them in full force as soon as possible. He might not be there for every game or recital but he will be there for the truly important times.

When the consistent man promises something, he means it. Only the most pressing of extenuating circumstances will knock him off the track he created with a promise.

One of the characteristics mentioned often by women when I ask them what defines a complete man is this consistency. They know they can count on their man to be where he is supposed to be when he is supposed to be there doing what he is supposed to be doing. This is not a matter of more often than not. You have to do much better than 51%. You have to set the bar very high. There needs to be no room for uncertainty. No number of excuses will make up for failure here.

Do whatever you have to do to track your promises and then keep them without fail or delay. Others will notice and like and trust you more and more.

20. The Complete Man Teaches Others

It is hard to understand why some men never want to share what they have personally discovered with others. I met a man who had some secrets on how to catch the big one when he went fishing. People constantly asked him to share but he refused. It was as if there was only one more fish to catch and it was reserved for him for his next day fishing. He figured out that I never fished and so one day he shared some of his secrets with me. Now I will never tell. Actually if I did probably I would leave out important details and you would be none the wiser anyway.

It is important and fulfilling to share what you know with others for their benefit. And if they really don't want to know then it probably isn't worth the sharing. But you build relationships with others by showing them how. There is no point in getting frustrated when people are slower to learn than you think they should be.

Everyone needs several steps. First of all the learner needs to watch or listen to you perform the skill in question. Then they need to try it themselves with you watching or listening. There is only one thing for sure, no matter how much they think they know what you know, they are bound to fail at their first attempt. Generally it takes at least six attempts before anyone starts to gather a skill for themselves. However, if all they are doing is repeating the same mistake over and over again they will never learn. As you are watching the person you are teaching you need to show them where they fail or are about to fail. And you need to do that with patience. What seems obvious to you will not seem obvious to your protege. You have to explain the process over and over. Eventually they will be ready to do it on their own when you are not watching. Again, there is only one thing you can know for sure. If you leave someone on their own to do a job they are going to blow it in all likelihood. Make sure that for the first several times you leave a learner on their own that it is a non-critical situation. It will take some time to get to where they need to be.

This process is never truer than with a father and son combination. Sons need to learn from their fathers. The things the son wants to learn may not be what the father wants to teach. The father has to start by teaching something that is of interest. You can encourage a son to learn from you but if he really doesn't want to there is very little you can do. Whipping him with words simply won't work. It is fascinating that fathers who were bullied by their fathers and berated with words have very little confidence and readiness to try almost anything. But at the same time they tend to replicate the useless technique with their own sons. This faulty process is easily more caught than taught. The good news is that a good father has an easier time passing on what he should if his own father was a good teacher. You can break the cycle if your own father was ineffective. On the other hand, you can learn from your effective father. The choice to learn is yours. When you teach your children well they appreciate it much more than you can know while they are children. The greatest relationships in life may be those between a good parent and an adult child. All the repeated efforts in their childhood may reap decades of benefit if you learn what you are doing.

What if you don't have children to teach? That is easy! There are many other children who need your help. Just open your eyes and start with someone else's child. Men in particular are in short supply to form healthy relationships with the children from homes where there is no father present.

The world needs men who teach. Men need to be taught by other men. Teenagers need to be taught by men. Children need to be taught by men. You can be the man!

21. The Complete Man Rests

If you set high aspirations for yourself you may fall subject to the fallacy that it is a badge of honour to run at such a pace that you get little sleep. I remember one such Christian leader who observed that he didn't need much sleep and could get by on four hours a night. He died young because human bodies aren't capable of that schedule.

Sleep is important. Very important. I have read about fifty books on sleep and I know there is some disagreement among researchers and experts but they all agree that if you don't get proper sleep your life span will be shortened. So you need to learn how to sleep.

Here are a few basic truths about sleep.

Three enemies of good sleep are nicotine, alcohol and caffeine. None of them help you sleep and all of them inhibit sleep to one degree or another.

Being overweight hurts your capacity to sleep properly. That too will kill you in time – often before you meet your grandchildren. Deal with it.

You must turn off all stimulation about two hours before you need to get to sleep. Generally that means you must turn off the electronics, the loud music and the lights.

Sleep in total darkness. Put garbage bags or tinfoil over your windows if you must. No light at all is best.

If you fall asleep in less than ten minutes you are not a good sleeper; you are sleep deprived.

If you have a hard time falling asleep you probably need to learn to put on paper what you are thinking about and tell yourself this isn't the time to deal with that. Your note will remind you in the morning. You may be too anxious. Figure it out.

If you wake up in the middle of the night and can't get back to sleep you may be showing signs of depression. Get some help but don't depend on medication. If you don't get back to sleep in twenty minutes get up and read something uplifting under dim light until you get sleepy.

If your mattress is more than about six years old replace it. And don't skimp on the quality. With a good mattress you won't toss and turn. Get a king sized bed if you sleep with a spouse. You can roll over on a king and not have to spin like you do on a double or queen. Bumping your partner is bad for both of you.

You need five or preferably six good cycles of sleep every night. I won't get too technical here but simply put your brain goes through four phases in one sleep cycle. Each phase has a different brain wave pattern. One of the four restores your body and another refreshes your mind. The last phase is when you dream during REM sleep – Rapid Eye Movement. That phase happens when you are not in deep sleep but almost awake. You get to a near awake stage at the end of REM sleep and either wake up or are easily aroused. Each cycle takes a specific amount of time. The average is about 90 minutes. So, six cycles is nine hours and five is seven and a half. If your personal cycle is longer you need more sleep to get to five or six and if it is shorter you need less. My personal cycle is an hour and ten minutes. So six cycles for me is seven hours. For my wife it is much longer.

You can figure out your cycle by tracking the time when you are aware you wake up in the night. If you go to sleep at 11 p.m. and find yourself briefly awake at 12:10 a.m. that would measure one cycle. But if you awake at 1:20 a.m. that would be too long for one cycle so you know it was two. By tracking yourself for a few nights you will figure out your personal cycle.

Forget depending on an alarm clock. Govern the time you need to wake up by the time you go to sleep.

Create good habits. Learn how to sleep properly. You will live longer!

22. The Complete Man Gets Angry

A nger is one of the most useful emotions. And anger misused is most destructive.

Anger management is one of the most powerful tools on the planet. Proper anger management is not simply developing a set of tools to stop yourself from destructive anger. However, having and using those tools is absolutely critical if you are going to be a complete man.

I don't want to dwell on inappropriate expressions of anger here as important as that subject is. Everyone knows how anger creates capacity for powerful expression. And when a man gets that wrong he creates a world of hurt and damage from which he may never fully recover. So this part of anger management is very important. But I want to look at something else.

You need to get angry about a lot of things. You need to get angry about your own self-centredness and selfish ambitions. If you don't get disgusted with yourself you aren't paying attention to the active and passive sin in your life. Personal anger over what Satan wants to do in and through you is a very good emotion. Get mad at the devil working in you. There is a myth about the great reformer Martin Luther getting so mad at the devil that he threw an ink well at him and hit the wall. Probably that story is not based in reality but the concept of Luther hating the temptations and the work of Satan on him is consistent with his general life. He was willing to take on big foes.

How about getting angry at one or two of the multitude of injustices in the world? I won't bother naming any because there are so many. If one of these stirs you up then get active and do something about it. Don't fall into the trap of believing your voice doesn't matter. It does matter to the people around you. It may not make a huge difference in the broad sense but you can make a big difference within your own network. People need to know where you stand and what you intend to do about it. There is a cause out there that needs your involvement.

If you know me, you already know that I will assert that the greatest cause in the world is the local church. Some have never thought about this but if Jesus is the smartest man who ever lived – and he is – then the things that stirred him should be the things that stir us. Jesus died for the church according to Paul (Ephesians 5:26). Did he make a mistake? Was it worth it? Sadly in some cases we don't see the churches we know making a difference. However, when a church gets it right, even though only 20% of the men come close to doing their part, that church makes a difference in the society. It fixes people and the people fix various problems in the community.

Don't waste your psychic fuel getting angry at the other people in church because they are passive or resting on their laurels. Just be the man that sets the example for others and a few will be inspired to be like you.

Don't personalize your anger on anyone. You will diminish your personal power if you get angry at people and hold a grudge as a regular pattern. You can do much more by being an example than you could ever be pointing out how others fail.

Get angry. But get angry about the correct things. Then do something to improve the situation.

23. The Complete Man Cares About Spiritual Things

Guys worry about being attractive. The outside matters some. But the really attractive part is the inside. Look in the mirror to see the inside of your soul. That is where the attractive part truly resides. Yes, you must take care of your body. Clean and neat count. Excess weight really hurts. Weak muscles are not impressive. However, no amount of grooming, styling and working out will make you attractive. Attractiveness comes from the inside.

In researching for this book I have asked many women what they think makes a complete man. The question stumps many. Then they often tell me there is no such man. Most women I meet "on the street" are disillusioned and hardened because men have let them down – repeatedly. Many women have learned the hard way that a man can pretend he is sensitive and caring so that he can get the one thing that is really on his mind. Seriously guys, is sex that important? Are you willing to just play a game and pretend you are something you are not to get it? If she hasn't figured out yet that you are just manipulative she will pretty soon. Then you are not just in the rough, you are in the deep weeds and may never recover. Fix your heart and do it now before you lose the game of life! The game of life is no game.

The core issue is that you must care about eternity. Jesus left this solid instruction, *"Do not store up for yourselves treasures on earth, where moth and rust destroy, and where thieves break in and steal. But store up for yourselves treasures in heaven, where moth and rust do not destroy, and where thieves do not break in and steal. For where your treasure is there will your heart be also."* (Matthew 6:19-21) So? Which part of that are you missing? On the one hand you get moths and rust to eat at your stuff and thieves to steal it. On the other hand you get heavenly permanence.

The first principle here is that you will store something somewhere. Will it be tools in the workshop, toys in the man cave or software games on the computer? Or will you take the long view and invest your time, talents and treasures on the other side of the grave? You pick.

The second factor is that you can't see what you are storing up in heaven in advance. It takes some faith to believe what you do for Jesus really matters for eternity because you don't always win when you work on the spiritual things on earth.

However, you inspire admiration, respect, joy, comfort and a whole host of other wonderful values when you try. What is most attractive to others is not that you are a winner but that you are a constant and consistent trier. You multiply that attraction when you give yourself to the eternal.

The reason the women I talk to on the street don't think there is a complete man is probably that they haven't met any men like the men I know who are consistently working on the eternal. None of these guys work on the spiritual for the sole purpose of becoming attractive but they get that attractiveness thrown in for free.

Some men assume that getting religion is a girl thing. Not! Real men benefit in every way when they take the lead in the spiritual realm. Give it a try. You will be amazed at how much your life is enhanced!

24. The Complete Man Promotes Peace

Guys often love to tell you what is wrong with the world. They can opine on what is wrong with the politician, the athlete, the boss, their wife and their children all in one sentence. They get frustrated that their complete explanations of how the world should operate are seldom taken to heart by others.

Any fool can find fault. It takes a complete man to find and implement solutions.

One of the components to creating solutions is to understand the problems in the first place. The other person's perspective on a problem is important – whether or not their viewpoint is correct or incorrect. When you can demonstrate that you understand where the other person is coming from you create the grounds for improvement. When you explain the other person's viewpoint to a third person it goes a long way to promoting understanding. When you understand then you are often given a listening ear.

Turn that around for a moment and think about the people you respond to. The people you resist and feel combative with are those you don't think understand your viewpoint. It is not so much that they hold a different view as it is that you are convinced they don't understand what you understand. The only way to get in step with each other is to start by proving you care about their viewpoint.

Peaceful relationships always start with this readiness to understand. People find it hard to understand each other. However when they do, they enjoy being with each other. If people don't enjoy being with you and you sense it then take a solid look at how much you are complaining about them or others. Learn to suspend your judgments until you understand more.

This works in the household. Screaming and hollering won't promote understanding. Even with the young child you will find them dropping their resistance when you listen to their concerns before you move on to explain why they can't have their own way.

Put yourself in the other person's shoes. Figure out why they are responding the way that they are. That person might believe there is a pattern in their life that is unfair. They might be right. Bend over and look at things from their perspective and you may see what they see. Then again, they might be wrong but when you are looking over their shoulder you are in a better position to point their eyes in a different direction so they can see a bigger picture.

See if you can run interference with issues that are difficult. All women want the people around them to pick up responsibilities and demonstrate that they do understand the circumstances. You don't have to do everything immediately if it is understood that you will do something later. But that can't be a vacant nebulous promise. The woman has to know you will get to it in the timely manner you promised.

A peaceful life begins at home. Peace at home begins with expectations that are met consistently. If you are compelled to complain about people you can diminish your angst by simply doing your part to create a happy peaceful environment wherever you are. And the best place to start is at home where you begin your day.

25. The Complete Man Controls A Lot

The title of this chapter might mislead you. It does not suggest that a complete man is controlling. It means that a man needs to take responsibility. If I said manages instead of controls that would fall short of the point.

Every man needs to be pro-active and adjust his vision so that he sees further down the road than the others in his household. This is true of the minutes and hours in a day but it is equally true of the weeks and months. Ultimately it is true of the years. All of these phases need to be kept in balance.

Some men control money with a tight fist and over plan for the future that will always be unknown. Money won't take care of all contingencies. Money for the future won't make you happier. Money is only useful when it is used, not when it is stockpiled. Take reasonable heed for the future but don't make the mistake so many do of trying to live there before it happens.

Some guys waste money on the frivolous. Some even blow money on predictable destruction. You don't have a dollar to waste on anything. Quit rationalizing away your money. Learn to save up for things you need. Realize that if you didn't need it when you left the house you still don't need it in the store even if it is on sale. But there is much more for a man to take charge of than his money. Time is the biggee. Men, track your time wasters. You can always get your hands on another dollar if you waste one. But you can never get your hands on another hour when you waste it. Killing time is the worst sort of murder you will ever commit. Simply don't do it.

The Complete Man

Some apparent time wasters turn out to be great investments when you walk in a life of faith and sincerely desire to use the time you have for Jesus. The impact of a meaningful conversation that happens seemingly at random and thus put you off your schedule may in fact be life changing for you or a friend. Make the best of your time. Control it.

You must take control of your brain power. You can do much more than you think you can. Stretch your brain in positive directions. Your brain is like a muscle; it works best with lots of exercise.

Take control of what you talk about. Clean up the subject matter and not just the words. Talk about what matters in this world. When others around you waste their words on lustful and venomous thoughts change the subject to something uplifting. Take charge. Here is some straight talk on talk. *"Those who consider themselves religious and yet do not keep a tight rein on their tongues deceive themselves, and their religion is worthless."* (James 1:29)

Take control of how you look and dress. Single guys are notorious at look-ing and even smelling like slobs. They are simply not aware of how they come across to others and how important that is. Mamma isn't there to dress them and they don't have a partner to keep them in line. Men often don't know they stink and look messy. Guys, this is basic: take a daily bath, shave, wear deodorant and take care of your teeth and complexion. Oh yes, teeth – brush them at least twice a day but you only need to floss the teeth you plan to keep! If you need false teeth find a way to afford them. Take control.

You won't get very far trying to control other people so don't waste your time. If you are an example of self-control others will be inspired by you and a few will follow you.

Men, take control of what you can to make a positive difference in your world. Quit drifting like the people you see around you who don't get it. Take a look at the losers if you like and take notes on how not to live! You were destined to win in life by being a man of control.

26. The Complete Man Stops Bullies

Bullying has become an important topic in recent years. I don't suspect that bullying has increased but our awareness of it has. Bullying isn't something that just happens with kids in the school yard or in social media. It is common among adults as well but is usually more sophisticated.

Men need to notice bullying behaviour and hold the bully to account. There will be times when bullying needs to be confronted in front of a group because bullies usually choose to do their work in front of others. Often they use unwitting accomplices asserting their agreement. This gives them the opportunity to say, "A number of us have been talking about this and ..." Such an approach is difficult to combat sensitively in a group context. Pre-emptive elimination of bullying is the best approach. When you recognize what is starting to happen you can stop the bully by personal one-on-one confrontation. The bully is usually actually a coward attempting to appear significant and brave.

The bully's main objective is to make someone feel small and inadequate. The main attack is always against the person's self-esteem or competence. The bully is not concerned with real issues. Bullies seek to remove the people that stand in their way.

The advanced technique of a bully is to pretend they are on the side of the one they intend to bully. They give that person lots of compliments and tell them how significant they are. Then when least expected they attack. The formula goes like this, "I used to believe thus and so but now you have totally destroyed your credibility with me. I am so disappointed because I thought you were better than that."

Bullies are sneaky; they use advance then retreat tactics. One quick punch may be followed by a pat on the back. They use body language to their advantage; they roll their eyes; they cross their arms; they let out loud sighs; they make sarcastic comments with deep meaning; then they say, "It was just a joke" if someone calls them on it. They act wounded and explain how they were being misunderstood.

Look for these seven types of bully. 1. The Loudmouth who speaks too much and at too great a volume. 2. The Quietmouth who acts like they are the one being bullied. Their main claim will be that they haven't been heard on the subject. 3. The Spokesperson who claims to advocate for a significant part of the group. 4. The Humiliator who uses condescending and demeaning language in reference to the person bullied. They treat their victims with destain. 5. The Questioner who poses his position or accusation in the form of a question that implies an answer. This gives them plausible deniability to say, "I was just asking." 6. The Bipolar who at one time acts like the person's best friend and then at another time flips from being positive to negative. 7. The Spiritualizer is my personal favourite. The Spiritualizer will tell you he has special knowledge because he prayed about it and heard from God on the matter.

Perhaps you would do well to look in the mirror and assess if you are ever a bully but never really realized it.

The best way to stop a bully in their tracks is to catch them early in the process and have a friendly chat to suggest their approach may be bordering on bullying or perceived that way by someone else. Above all if you know in your heart things are not right, stand up to the bully. Look the bully in the eyes and be assertive but not aggressive. When they interrupt don't lose your place. Get back on your agenda; don't let them hijack the conversation. Don't respond to taunts and challenges in kind. Just respectfully and directly make your point. When you have confidence that the bullying is becoming dangerous inform your superiors because they need to know in order to notice.

Stop bullying in its tracks. Don't leave it up to others. Have the courage to follow up on your convictions.

27. The Complete Man Advocates for Others

There is a time when a good man simply needs to stay out of the way and not get involved. If there is no way you can or should become a part of the solution then getting involved will only make you part of the problem. However, more often than not it is easy to err on the other side. Too much passivity is what drives women nuts. They want their man to show some engagement in the right things at the right time.

One of the key factors for a man to decide if he should get involved is whether or not the situation and need is right there in his pathway. It may be a good idea to ignore some things that are happening at a distance but problems right in front of you must be dealt with in some way.

You may recall the story of the Good Samaritan. (Luke 10:25-27) It addresses the question of when one should get involved. It is the story Jesus uses to answer the question, "Who is my neighbour?" The question wasn't really designed to be a question because the expert in the law was really trying to cover his butt. What he really was attempting to communicate was the old, "There are so many hurting neighbours out there I can't help them all. And if I helped a few that would be leaving the others out so it would be showing favouritism." Jesus pretended that the question was real and not a smokescreen for non-involvement in the world. There are two bad guys and one good guy in the story. The two bad guys avoided the man who had been attacked and walked on by. It was the man from Samaria (that's a zinger because Jews thought Samaritans were worthless or second class at best) who dealt with the problem right in his path.

That shouldn't be complicated to understand. If the problem sticks itself right in your face you should probably deal with it. You don't have to get off the road from Jerusalem to Jericho and find the road from Jerusalem to Gaza unless you are Philip. (See Acts 8:26) It is the road you are on right now that matters. You have plenty of people on your road that need your attention. Someone else has the assignment of the next road over. You have to take that in faith. To be sure, God may interrupt your pattern and put you on another road. He does that. But for now, you are not on a vacant highway. There are people right in your path you need to stick up for.

It isn't the absence of opportunity that is your problem; it is insensitivity to the opportunity God has given you. Don't wake up every day asking God to give you opportunity. He already has you on Opportunity Street. Wake up asking the Lord to make you sensitive to the opportunity under your nose. Sometimes you will miss the opportunity because the person you need to advocate for won't be displaying gaping wounds. The person may be covering his wounds in a three piece suit by Armani.

A friend of mine has a factory in China even though he lives down the street from me. On Skype one night he told me how he was walking the streets of Xiamen, China on a Sunday asking the Lord for an assignment because the English church meeting had been canceled. A man with a young seemingly lifeless boy laid him on the street in front of him. Hundreds watched. Nobody jumped in to help. By using mouth-to-mouth resuscitation which is unknown in China, my friend kept the boy alive and revived him before the police and an ambulance arrived. Dramatic but real.

Open your eyes and help someone today. You can figure that out. Ask God to make you aware of who you can help. Something to do may come to mind. Do it. Someone may ask for your help. Help them. You don't need to be a bystander any more.

28. The Complete Man Leads His Family

Somewhere along the line our western society lost its way. You probably believe that. I would submit to you for your consideration that the problem starts with the family. You probably believe that the basic building block of society is the family. But perhaps you are like most men who are rather fuzzy on where to go from there.

The problem is not that the men don't bring home the bacon. It goes deeper. The problem is not that men don't take charge. That is a simplistic failing view of leadership. The problem is that men don't provide the leadership they should. Leadership has been studied from many directions. Most men continue to make rookie mistakes by attempting to dominate their family members under the guise of leadership. If you have been working on that approach may I ask how that's working out for you? Not so good, huh? So what will you do?

Leadership requires you gathering the appropriate relevant information and doing research. It requires that you share what you are learning as you learn it. It requires that you talk over what you are learning with trusted advisers. If you don't have a coach or mentor you will stay near the back of the pack. You need to talk. Talking is the doing part of thinking. And you don't need to talk just to convince everyone how right you are. You need to factor in every objection to your thinking that you hear.

If your partner just pushes back when you raise the possibility of a new direction in your life then something is wrong. Assume for the moment that it is wrong in you – not in her. You need to hear her concerns without just putting up your dukes. Make sure you understand the factors that she raises. Further, you must understand the weight she places on the factor. For example, you might think changing her favourite store should be no big deal but if it is to her, then you have to face that challenge carefully. You won't lead by simply telling her how wrong she is in caring about that. Without interrogating like you were in a court room you must find out what is important piece by piece. Let's say it is the store thing. We used to have a grocery store that bragged, "It's mainly because of the meat." Some people shopped elsewhere because for them it was mainly because of something else. It could have been location, parking, cleanliness, selection, price, staff and so on. Your issue probably isn't shopping but it does have similar factors. When you understand the factors you can move forward by pointing out other compensating factors or eliminating problems another way.

I am writing this chapter in the car while Wendy shops for groceries. That isn't the normal pattern. She almost always does the shopping but what is different today is that one windshield wiper broke on the passenger's side of the car. It isn't raining and if it did she would still have the most important wiper if she drove herself. But she asked if I could drive her. I quickly agreed to change my schedule. I needed a secluded spot to write a chapter. I intended to do that later today. But it was no big deal for me to adapt. Now when it comes to something that needs more discussion I have some good will in the bank I may need to use up at another time when Wendy gives a little.

I could never be a leader in our home if I always insisted that Wendy do all the adapting. She is quite adaptable when I give her enough lead time to figure things out.

Become the adaptable man who sets aside his own agenda for others. And make sure your family gets all the attention they need from you.

29. The Complete Man Achieves A Lot

I have attended and even conducted my share of funerals. Everyone knows that at funerals people try to say nice things about the departed person. It always gives me a knot in my gut when I realize that all those words amount to a cover up. A few pleasant incidents or characteristic from the person's life mask the fact that there isn't much good to say.

The words of an old Paul Simon tune say, "I am a citizen of the planet / I was born here / I'm going to die here / Come what may ..." The words go on to speak of the notion that by virtue of birth everyone is entitled to the treasures of the earth and must not be denied them. He missed the bull's eye by several rings. Yes, we all live and will all die. Yes, there are untold treasures on this earth. But when you add in that we are all created in the image of God it gives every man a stewardship that is much more than a live and let live destiny.

You and I are here to be somebody. We are here to do something that lasts beyond our meagre lifetime. We impact people who will in turn impact other people we may never meet. If our impact is small or negative we will pass on the predisposition to be small for generations to come. The world doesn't need small men. When a man sets his highest aspiration to work for "the man" for a few decades so he can feed his family and then go off and play in the sandboxes he created for when the kids are gone, has missed his life's meaning.

You are here to put in more than you take out. Do you get that? You can do much more than build a nice castle in the sky with a pretty white picket fence. You are here to make a difference for people. The greatest resource on the planet is human potential. You have your share. You can muddle through the maze of opportunities and leave a mark that outlives you. But you can only do that if you take the time to ponder and observe. Find the needs right in front of you, pick up the tools of human potential and do something. You may not be the one to own the patent to the solution for world hunger. You may not be the prime mover to get a cathedral built. You may not even be the man who supervises something that the world notices. But you can be much more than the man on the street with the best lawn or the cleanest car.

Let's get specific. You can take up the cause of a Sunday School class of boys who need a solid man in their life. You can send out a thoughtful encouraging message every day to someone who could use a little encouragement. You can offer to help someone fix something that is staring them in their face but they simply don't know how to get it fixed. You can go out of your way to buy a coffee for a man who has left his impression on the end of the couch where he sits hours every day. He probably has a remote or two on the arm of the couch that is covered with the grease left over from the chips he dropped and couldn't find the energy to pick up. Everyone knows he is the definition of "couch potato" but there is a good chance nobody lovingly shows him that the root cause of his state in life is his own laziness and not that he never gets a break. Maybe nobody has told him you make your own breaks. Probably he doesn't know that and needs to hear it repeated several times.

Such human engagements may not get noted by others. However, those who give up things in favour of serving Jesus and spreading the Gospel are the ones who will be at the front of the line when the final accounting is done. That is because every man has the opportunity to achieve much more than all the people behind him in the line achieve.

Don't wish for a better opportunity. Make the best of the opportunity you have today. Then in the end you will have lived a productive life and have achieved much more than you ever thought possible.

30. The Complete Man Gives

Moms, girlfriends, fiancés and wives always want the men in their lives to give of themselves. They donate their time. They donate their interests. They donate their money.

Someone said that the difference between men and boys is the price of their toys. Don't spend so much money on toys. You are not going to impress any woman with your new video game or your new snowmobile or boat. Don't invest your life in your toys; invest your life in your people. Am I against all these nice things? No, but don't invest yourself there. Give of yourself in such a way that the women in your life get what they want in their lives long before you get what you prefer. Don't bother to keep score. That is very unimpressive. You know what I mean. "Awww you got to go out with the girls to shop once so I should be allowed to blow two events with the boys to break even." That is the land war in Asia you should be smart enough to stay out of.

John Wesley (1703-1791) once said, "Earn all you can; give all you can; save all you can." He didn't mean he thought you should create a money pile. He meant you should be frugal. Once he said this, "If I leave behind me ten pounds [when I die]... you and all mankind bear witness against me, that I have lived and died a thief and a robber." He gave away a boatload of money during his lifetime. You can too. But not if you don't earn it and not if you think it is important to pile it up.

Francis Bacon (1561-1626) wrote some things I wish I had said first. "Money is a great servant but a bad master." My fav is, "Money is like manure, of very little use except it be spread." I only missed being first by a few centuries.

These are timeless truths men. Worry about your eternal portfolio, not the amount you have set aside under a mattress in the stock market. Over the years I have met several men who strut over what they give. I have come to understand that those who want to brag about how much they give actually don't give as much as they pretend. There may be some exceptions. I haven't found one yet.

If you want financial prosperity one of the keys is to give 10% or more of your gross income to the Lord's work through your local church. Everyone who does will testify that their 90% goes further than the 100% for those who don't trust God with money. You will never beat God giving. He makes money abound when you give it all to Him and demonstrate that you put Him first in your money. Pay God back first and let the bank stand in line for the mortgage payment. You will never run short when you manage money God's way.

If you wait until you have money left over to give you will never give. Give on the front end because it is priority and see what happens. What is the worst thing that can happen if you do? You might have to make some downward adjustments in your giving to pay a bill or two. I have never met a man that told me he had to do that. Maybe you will be the first. Don't waste what is left after you give and you will find that you probably end up just fine. That's my story. I'm sticking to it. And as I say, "Do I look like I'm starving?"

Men don't like it when someone tells them how to spend their money. How about you? If this chapter gives you heartburn then probably you need to change the money flow. You don't need an antacid. You need a financial adjustment. There will never be a better time than now!

31. The Complete Man Prays

If you waste your life praying to gods of wood and stone you will end up disappointed. But if you invest in prayer to the Triple-Unified God of Heaven you will see some benefits.

The first thing you may notice about the results of true prayer is that it settles your soul. I never met a man getting up off his knees who had a chip on his shoulder. You can't keep a chip on your shoulder while you are on your knees for very long.

When a man prays with his eyes closed it opens the eyes of his soul. It gives him a broader perspective.

Ideas pop into your head when you are praying. The first set of ideas are the sinful red herrings Satan draws across your path. While you might not know how diversionary they are when you are in a mental state of non-prayer you most certainly will when you are praying. It is not wrong to be tempted. That is inevitable. It is a bad idea to mull over the temptation. If you let your mind ask, "Will I or won't I?" you are on a very slippery slope and may lose your footing faster than you imagine.

However, other ideas will pop into your head while you are praying. Take these as from the Lord. For example, you could be praying about a difficult situation and asking God to point you to a solution. You might be surprised by a possible solution popping into your head or more often than that, you might think of someone who can help you form the solution you need.

Our emphasis in prayer is far too often to pray about what we think we need God to do for us and be done with it. Guys, God is not your butler. He is your Master. Never forget that when you ask. Ask in the right way and with the right motives and you will be amazed how many positive solutions show up.

When you pray start by recalling to your mind all the great things God has done for you. Don't focus on the material blessings but don't leave them out either. If you don't think you have been blessed with material blessings get on a plane to somewhere where the GDP per capita is about 10% of yours and you will get a very loud wake up call.

Remember the non-tangible blessings first. If you know Jesus then you will be hard pressed to get through a prayer session and not remember to thank him for your salvation.

When you pray don't forget to come before God with a humble attitude and once again ask him for his forgiveness. Private sins require a private confession; others don't need to know how smelly your garbage is. You really miss the mark on two things every day. You do things you shouldn't do and you leave things out you should have included. The complete man doesn't compare himself to someone else; he takes a good look in the mirror.

Real men speak up in group prayer meetings. They don't know all the formulations of words that make them sound smart or theological. They just talk to God out loud in the presence of others. This activity is a great encouragement. Pray out loud with the males and the females in your life. If you haven't figured it out yet the women you love like your voice and they really like it when they hear you talking to God.

It could be that you have always treated prayer as a useless activity. Check out the facts. You can Google "results of prayer" and see 100,000 web pages. They won't all be equally valuable but you will find that prayer is anything but useless.

Capture some time for careful and thoughtful prayer and you will see the difference prayer can make.

32. The Complete Man Takes Care of His Health

Some things are complex. The human body is amazingly complex. My youth sponsor when I was a teenager came to Christ at medical school. He told me that when he started to study the complexity of the human body it convinced him there must be a God. And that was over fifty years ago when comparatively speaking medical science was in its infancy. We know much more about that complexity today.

Men, yes, you have your genetics. Yes, you have the habits you formed based on the habits of your family of origin. But you can take care of what you have left.

This part is simple.

Eat properly. I am not a nutritionist but I have had more than one man tell me how he eats properly but he doesn't eat fruits and vegetables. I seldom bother to point out the nonsense. I just change the subject. Personally I have found that every dime I have invested in the good food we can't afford has been worth it. Wendy and I are not health food fanatics. Winston Churchill said, "A fanatic is one who can't change his mind and won't change the subject." We have observed that all our friends are on multiple medications and we aren't. They think we got lucky. Maybe. We think it is because we pay more attention.

Sleep properly. I covered that in chapter 21. Seriously, you need to work on it. If you snore loudly it is an indication something is wrong. If you carry excess weight you undoubtedly snore and you are prone to sleep apnea.

Start by putting a wedge under the head of your mattress and raise the upper part of your body about six inches. That might make a difference. Not attending to your snoring problem will do damage to your marriage, not just yourself.

Establish as stable a routine as possible. That can be difficult with varying schedules. But don't just do what you need to do when you feel like it. Make it your pattern to be consistent with the things that stand to improve your health. If a doctor tells you to do something or take some medication, just do it. The doctor isn't always right but you will be far better off if you fail the doctor's way first.

Exercise. According to Dan Buettner in his well researched book *The Blue Zones* natural exercise beats the unnatural machine and class type exercise by a considerable margin. I am not great on this point but I know that when I am working fixing stuff at my house or helping someone else do something physical I am way healthier. I find that when I get out there and do something physical I lose a few pounds and gain a much greater mental clarity. If you do that you will find the same results.

Of course, there are other health things to talk about. Don't over complicate it. Eat. Sleep. Exercise. Then your next visit to the doctor will be more of a victory celebration than a visit to the principal's office.

33. The Complete Man Is Trustworthy

Trustworthiness is shown in many characteristics. It simply means that people can trust you to be the same in all circumstances. The complete man is worthy of trust. People need to know you will do what you said you would do when you said you would do it. You might think your excuses make sense but others probably don't.

There are other characteristics that build trust. For example, demonstrate consideration to others and you will be trusted more. Women respond to that. Don't you want your children, your wife, all those around you to be considerate? You want others to help you when you need it. You want someone to pay attention when things are not going so well for you and demonstrate some concern and interest in your life. You need to deliver the same trustworthiness.

Complete men listen with their ears, their eyes and their heart. Statements like, "Yah, I got you (as they stand texting their friend)" and "You don't have to finish – I know what you are going to say" aren't going to cut it.

Keep your promises. "Mom, I'll do my homework as soon as ..." "Did you get your homework done?" " Well, that is what I was going to do next." Is it the same thing now that you have graduated to adulthood? "Would you mind taking out the garbage?" "Yah, yah, just after the game is over!" The game is not important; the garbage is. Keep your promises. Become a "do it now" person. Don't postpone things. There will be something else that intervenes 20 minutes or 20 days from now so don't wait for spare time. It probably won't come your way. Make it a habit to be a "do it now" person and that shows honour to others. Make them proud. If your mom wasn't a "do it now" person, you know the results of it. Always keep your promises to your mother, to your fiancé or wife, to your children, to your friends and to others. It is a great characteristic.

Tell the truth – even when it hurts. Don't lead others to believe something that is not true even though you don't directly lie. Leave the correct impression and don't just skirt an issue. Be direct. If a so-called diplomatic answer evades the truth at a time when the truth should be laid out, people will remember later when they find out that you knew something but didn't declare it in a timely matter. Don't convey one message to one person because they want to hear it while you convey a different message to another person. When the two compare notes they will know you have a hard time being consistent with facts and that will diminish or even destroy their trust in you.

When you say you have something covered you had better have it covered. Don't hope things will be all right; make them right. You have met men who are so smooth with their talk that the boss believes them but you know they are blowing smoke. Don't be like those slippery souls.

People are far more likely to forgive your mistakes and sins if you admit it when you blow it. Everyone doesn't need to know all the details of your failings. Even those closest to you don't need to know absolutely everything but they do need to know that you won't be guilty of a cover up when a more open declaration is called for. You have to be careful not to say too much and particularly too much too soon. However, when some fact comes to light those who trust you need to know the fact at the correct time before it is too late.

You want people to trust you. You might start with attributed trust that comes with the brass nameplate on the door. But if you aren't trustworthy it will catch up with you. I have never seen the status symbol of a beautiful nameplate with a title on a bedroom door. The people you live with know the truth. Be the man you told the world you were in your resume.

34. The Complete Man Has Spring in His Step

There is nothing more boring than a draggy man. A man who whines and moans about every ache and pain is very unattractive.

The other day Wendy and I were getting on a plane that had been delayed. She went to a seat at the back and I was at the front. The flight attendant was a little flustered and apologized. Another man and I on one side of the aisle both commented that there was no reason for us to complain and everything was just fine. But the man across the aisle from me said, "With the amount of flying I do, I have the right to complain." The flight attendant looked him in the eye and quietly said, "I guess that gives me the right to complain then, does it?" I quickly jumped in between and responded with a twinkle in my eye, "Oh no, you get paid to listen to complainers." Of course, that isn't even close to true. Now guess. How is that complaining man in the rest of his life? What would you vote for, complete or incomplete? Oh, you know what his wife thinks without ever having met either of them. Apparently the man has no shock absorbers. He was no fun at all. But the rest of us were making it a good time.

What if you don't have a spring in your step? What if life is a constant drag? There are two things to consider.

The first is this. Life sucks. No really. It does. And you are going to hit some snags along the way. *"Yet man is born to trouble as surely as sparks fly upward."* (Job 5:7) This truth is written in what may be the oldest book of the Bible by the man who had a lot more trouble than you or me. Guys, when you are cruising along without thought, trust me, before you are done you are going to get slapped, slugged or gob-smacked by something or someone. And what's more is that it won't be a one and done situation. There will be more to come. So get ready. When the burglar breaks the glass to get in your house it is not the time to go out to the garage to pump iron so you can fight him off. As for the fact of trouble, it will happen. Ready or not.

However, if you are the complete man people will marvel over your true joy in life. It won't be the fake joy of denial or positive thinking. It will be a joy from deep in your soul that gives you a sense of humour until your dying breath. That is only possible if you trust in Jesus Christ alone and completely for your eternal salvation and for your driving force for life on earth. I mentioned before this quote from Jesus. Jesus was clear, *"The thief comes only to steal and kill and destroy; I have come that they may have life, and have it to the full."* (John 10:10). Was he selling something and overstating the value? Or was he telling the truth? You have to decide.

The second thing about a spring in your step is this. Happiness is a choice. Sunrises are as real as train wrecks. Concentrate on the sunrises. At the beginning of your day decide it is going to be a good one regardless of what comes your way. Make the best use of the inevitable train wrecks. You can only do that if you live your days with the beauty of the sunrise and sunsets as your focal point. Notice the smile of a child. Look at the beauty of the green trees meeting the blue sky. Pick a flower and smell its fine fragrance Taste a berry and savour the flavour. Take a deep breath and feel the stresses melt away. This is a day. This is the day. This is the only day you have for today. *"The stone the builders rejected* [later to be clearly known as Jesus] *has become the cornerstone; the Lord has done this, and it is marvelous in our eyes. The Lord has done it this very day; let us rejoice today and be glad."* (Psalm 118:22-24)

If that can't put a spring in your step I have nowhere else to send you. If you happen to be the guy on the plane who thinks he has a right to complain give yourself a shake!

35. The Complete Book

So that is pretty much it for now. I asked my wife to read it and give me her feedback. (If you found any typos blame it on her because she is my best proofreader.) But more than that I wanted to know if I hit the spot. Wendy said two things. The first was that there is a lot of good advice in here. And she was gracious enough to not mention that there are days when I need to take my own advice. The second thing was she said it is very complete. I think she missed it on that one. But it made me feel good anyway.

I started the book aiming at about twenty short chapters. I put my list out to many women I trust. Then it grew to about thirty chapters. Then it got to about forty or so. I cut back as you can see. But I am sure there are at least thirty more subjects I would like to cover.

The thing is this. This book is very incomplete. I know that. The chapters in here are in more or less random order. That was deliberate because I wanted to sneak up on you and not let you decide to skip a section.

The complete book is The Book – The Bible. That is where you can learn to become a complete man.

This week I learned that when a boy in Guyana climbs a coconut tree he will find the lower branches that are dead. When he opens a curled up leaf on that branch he will find caterpillars. Those caterpillars will be brown like the colour of the leaf they are taking their nourishment from. As he climbs further up the tree to the green branches he will find green leaves curled up with green caterpillars inside. Same species; different colour. They take on the colour of their nourishment. What a great story! It illustrated beautifully how life works for a man.

The Complete Man

If you decide to live in the Word of God – the Bible – slowly and imperceptibly to you, you will take on its colour. There is nothing better for you to do in life. You won't see the change happening as fast as you might wish – at least not usually. But over time you will change. You will grow and you will find a new heart. You will care about things you never dreamed would interest you. You will start to find the courage to back up the convictions that grow in your soul. Over time you will find yourself becoming what you really wanted to become in the first place. You want to be the complete man.

The cover of this book has a reproduction of *The Vitruvian Man* by Leonardo daVinci (1452-1519). It looks pretty accurate to me. At the time other artists didn't worry about getting the proportions perfect. DaVinci set a new standard by carefully measuring the ideal proportions. I don't think you should care nearly as much about your body as you do your inner parts. The men around you are probably very poorly proportioned on the inside. But if you set the standard in your world striving to be the complete man some will notice. Some men will start to come to you for advice. If you give them advice consistent with the Word of God they will appreciate it and some will join you in the walk of faith.

Make it your aim to know the Bible; be driven to live it out. Check everything I have said here with the Bible to make sure I didn't miss the target. You will be amazed at how complete you become in a year or two.

In a sentence, the complete man walks with God. Be that man!

Other Books

Kainos Enterprises through its publishing wing emphasizes themes, books and resources rarely available elsewhere and through a variety of platforms and media. Here are some books for you to consider.

See You Next Week is about welcoming and retaining newcomers into your church. Most churches are unaware that they could do much better at this. Learn the keys.

Gary V Carter & Robin W Pifer
www.SeeYouNextWeek.info

How to Reproduce Your Church is a practical guide for church leaders thinking about the possibility of extending their ministry by starting one or more daughter churches.

Timothy Starr & Gary V Carter
www.ChurchReproduction.info

Life on the Zipline is a practical guide for any individual who wants to maximize the one way trip from where they are to the end of the line.

Gary V Carter, Warwick Cooper, Robin W Pifer, Douglas Rowley
www.LifeontheZipline.com

How to Crank It Up – Without Getting Cranky is a penetrating and insightful book to walk leaders through the minefield of church leadership.

Gary V Carter
www.HowToCrankItUp.info

Look At The Birds and Consider The Wildflowers is a fresh look at the birds and flowers out Wendy's back window sprinkled with homey personal and family anecdotes.

Wendy E. Carter
www.LookAtTheBirds.info

Made in the USA
Charleston, SC
08 July 2015